WALKING OUT OF THE WORLD

Also by Matthew Mead

POETRY

Identities
The Administration of Things
The Midday Muse
A Sestina at the End of Socialism

TRANSLATIONS
(*with Ruth Mead*)

JOHANNES BOBROWSKI: Shadow Lands
MAX HÖLZER: Amfortiade
CHRISTA REINIG: The Tightrope Walker
HEINZ WINFRIED SABAIS: The People and the Stones

Matthew Mead

Walking Out of the World

AND OTHER POEMS

Anvil Press Poetry

Published in 2004
by Anvil Press Poetry Ltd
Neptune House 70 Royal Hill London SE10 8RF
www.anvilpresspoetry.com

This book is published with financial assistance
from The Arts Council of England

Designed and set in Monotype Bell by Anvil
Printed and bound in England
by Cromwell Press, Trowbridge, Wiltshire

ISBN 0 85646 365 5

A catalogue record for this book
is available from the British Library

WITH RUTH

Acknowledgements

Connections, Eavesdropper, The Frogmore Papers, Iota, Numbers, Oasis, PN Review, Scratch, Shearsman

The Frogmore Press for *A Dozen Villanelles* (1999)

Oasis Books for *The Sentences of Death* (2000)

Malcolm Rutherford for a poem from the Satis pamphlet *A Roman in Cologne*

Contents

The Sentences of Death

Invocation

The words are falling into place
Telling that you again return
As lucid as the shape of grace
The words are falling into place
Telling me I shall see your face
Where wildfires run and rumours burn
The words are falling into place
Telling that you again return.

Ancient & Modern: Five Poems

In Brief

Darkness deep upon the waters,
Nothing very much to do,
He imagined sons and daughters
Eerily like me and you.

Building paradise was easy,
Eden opened without fuss –
Somewhere for the bright and breezy;
Awfully, again, like us.

Fallcrashbang. The blissful banished.
Imagist and image gone.
Heaven knows what else has vanished.
We are standing here alone.

Who created the creator,
Called him god and let him die
Like his own impersonator?
Hellishly. Like you and I.

Below Zero

The night is dark, the kings have come,
Beasts breathe, bells ring and shepherds sprawl.
Our hearts are cold, our hands are numb,
We scarcely shiver now at all.

The hordes of earth are watching still
The progress of a single star.
A revelation of all ill
Sickens within the things that are.

A snowflake flicks the air again,
Footprints retrace the steps they trod,
And deep in drifts of chilly pain
An icy womb delivers god.

Into Avarice

Too many people want too much
What you exceed will provide excess
Jammed up tight to an easy touch
Multitudes make a multimess

Too many people chock the earth
Too many cradles creak in vain
You are a woman for all your worth
I am one of too many men

Not just the crush of all the idle
Too many people too many people
Also the fear of fratricidal
Too many people too many people

Multiply that which you have not got
By any number however small
Some of too many will want a lot
All of the others will want it all.

In the Changing Room

A light like light on land or sea,
The ashes and the earth around.
All that has been and is to be
Is lying level with the ground.

The resurrectors come and go,
Restarting hearts, restoring breath.
Lips murmur names they seem to know,
A cold tongue starts to count its teeth.

No drawn-out method will do now.
We want a way to make time fly,
A grin transforming mouth and brow,
Another twinkling of an eye.

We want him up, we want him quick,
A whiff of rubbing-oil and sweat –
A trainer with a team to pick.
We want to see some action yet.

The Brew

We knew the vintage sour but trod
And trusted that we need not taste
The bitter draught we brought the god.
He sipped and swallowed and grimaced.

A little we distilled, our fire
Ill-regulated, smouldered, burst
With fervours of a funeral pyre;
We filled the bottles, feared the worst.

Pour out the spirit of the age
And raise the cup which will not pass
That impotence again may rage
And dusty ciphers sneer 'Alas'.

A Dozen Villanelles

Villanelle of the Final Whole

for WJC

                                                         *

Horrible feet and horrible teeth   *teef*
The corn uncut and the biter bit
Old age is often a time of death   *deff*

The sort of day when you can't quite breathe   *breev*
When you can't quite stand and it hurts to sit
Horrible feet and horrible teeth   *teef*

Something is happening underneath   *underneef*
The underneath that you daren't admit
Old age is often a time of death   *deff*

A rusty sword as you catch your breath   *breff*
An icy stone in the stomach's pit
Horrible feet and horrible teeth   *teef*

This is the sky you lived beneath   *beneef*
Pressing you down beyond remit
Old age is often a time of death   *deff*

This is a grave and this a wreath   *wreef*
This is about the end of it
Horrible feet and horrible teeth   *teef*
Old age is often a time of death   *deff*

* rhymewords in native tongue

Villanelle of the Last Gasp

Put out the final cigarette
And do you really want that drink
Prepare to live and die in debt

The day is drained beyond regret
The glass is cracked the ashtrays stink
Put out the final cigarette

A dirty shirt a losing bet
You are not worth a jockey's wink
Prepare to live and die in debt

Whisky like water wet and wet
A cashflow on the rocks clink clink
Put out the final cigarette

The bedclothes will be wet with sweat
Pink elephants will all be pink
Prepare to live and die in debt

This lady dressed in stockinet
Will pour your whisky down the sink
Put out the final cigarette
Prepare to live and die in debt.

A Villanelle on Hold

I wrote a poem yesterday
naked as her next of kin
I shan't do very much today

With words as bright as breaking day
diamond nipple, scented skin
I wrote a poem yesterday

My lines still hold that fair array
Fräulein Flender smooth as sin
I shan't do very much today

In metaphors for come what may
Mrs Perkins drowned in gin
I wrote a poem yesterday

My time is lost beyond delay
virgin in a crinoline
I shan't do very much today

That's it then at the close of play
scaly hands are cold and thin
I wrote a poem yesterday
I shan't do very much today

Villanelle of the Unslept Night

A rainy wind will lash the pane
And I shall listen where I lie.
I shan't get back to sleep again.

I'll lie and hear the old refrain
Of empty buses going by.
A rainy wind will lash the pane.

Then up and out to slash and strain
And back to groan and snort and sigh:
I shan't get back to sleep again.

Noise and nocturia. In vain,
Like a relentless lullaby,
A rainy wind will lash the pane.

Some bits of night may still remain,
The dreamy bits where people die.
I shan't get back to sleep again

Before the dirty stain of dawn
Before I've even closed an eye
A rainy wind will lash the pane
I shan't get back to sleep again.

Villanelle of the Sudden Twinge

I felt the pain once more.
It may well go away.
It went away before.

A pang of something sore,
An echo of decay.
I felt the pain once more.

An achey pain, cocksure
Of coming night and day.
It went away before.

It creeps back to recur
Or jabs back in to stay.
I felt the pain once more.

The pill and shot and smear
All help and you can pray.
It went away before.

It gets to be a bore
But I can only say:
It went away before
I felt the pain once more.

An Unrhymed Villanelle

A villanelle without a rhyme
A clock that ticks no tick but tock
Like decommissioning the wheel

A massive miss a screeching brake
The mainspring snaps the hands stand still
A villanelle without a rhyme

It isn't true it can't be done
A clock that tells the time too late
Like decommissioning the wheel

The dark mechanic stops to stare
A clock that tells no time at all
A villanelle without a rhyme

The dark mechanic gets to work
I just don't care I just can't watch
Like decommissioning the wheel

Men shuffle down deserted roads
A dead sound on the stroke of ten
A villanelle without a rhyme
Like decommissioning the wheel.

A Double Villanelle

I have decreed the fortyeight hour day
And each dark hour shall lengthen thy delight;
The tempo is tomorrow's long delay.
My law of leisure idles time away
Making eternity an *Ewigkeit*;
Enjoy the whole of it on double pay.

You shall no longer live in disarray
Of fleeting moments or of sudden fright,
I have decreed the fortyeight hour day;
A minute circles like a bird of prey,
Hovers unswooping in a slowflap flight;
My law of leisure idles time away.

The status quo stands where it is to stay
For twice the time you ever thought it might.
The tempo is tomorrow's long delay
And clocks that you no longer need obey
Strike 'Never' in the middle of the night;
Enjoy the whole of it on double pay.

Who would not be immortal let him pray
To such swift gods who speed him from his plight.
I have decreed the fortyeight hour day –
A lump of time to play and then replay,
All out, stumps drawn, but no result in sight.
My law of leisure idles time away.

Dawn, double-spaced, has dawdled till midday
And luncheon found no end of appetite,
The tempo is tomorrow's long delay.
Unchanged, unaltered, not a hair turned gray,
Running to length in all you ever write –
Enjoy the whole of it on double pay.

A double villanelle, a negligée
Concealing nothing from a second sight.
I have decreed the fortyeight hour day.
The tempo is tomorrow's long delay.
A double villanelle and come what may
All loves endure, eternal flames burn bright;
My law of leisure idles time away,
Enjoy the whole of it on double pay.

Villanelle: A Blotted Weltanschauung

I only had my reading glasses on
And what I saw was quite a way away
And when I looked again the lot had gone.

I should have seen the whole thing seen as one
By eyes that flash beyond a dying day;
I only had my reading glasses on.

One steadfast gaze in detail might have done
To shape the scene. I blinked; a blinding ray;
And when I looked again the lot had gone.

What is believed is seen, the world is won
By eyes that pierce the distance like dismay.
I only had my reading glasses on.

What meets the eye is what the seer soon
Proclaims as faith. I felt a faith decay.
And when I looked again the lot had gone.

The naked girl was breasted like a swan
As my wife saw and as I heard her say
I only had my reading glasses on
And when I looked again the lot had gone.

slender
fine
tender

attend her
shrine
slender

send her
shine
tender

defender
thin
slender

splendour
wine
tender

surrender
mine
slender
tender.

Villanelle of the Last Lap

walking the final mile
with nothing left to say
smiling a toothless smile

one man in single file
trying to lose his way
walking the final mile

meeting a crocodile
of schoolgirls all gone grey
smiling a toothless smile

going on all the while
to while all time away
walking the final mile

claiming no domicile
drawn on beyond dismay
smiling a toothless smile

beyond the broken stile
stumbling back to stay
walking the final mile
smiling a toothless smile.

A Villanelle in Memory of Edward Mummery

You sail beyond the setting sun,
Hold course towards the final shore.
The water and the world are one.

Daring the dark to face alone
Uncharted seas uncrossed before
You sail beyond the setting sun.

A wind that tears, the tides that run,
A broken wave, the stormy roar,
The water and the world are one.

Above pearl eyes and coral bone,
The oozy depths, the mermaid's lure,
You sail beyond the setting sun.

You are the man you made your own.
The land is drowned to dry no more.
The water and the world are one.

You make the voyage, never done,
To morning like a golden door.
You sail beyond the setting sun.
The water and the world are one.

A Badly Bloated Villanelle

A truth that we shall never know
In words we do not want to hear,
A sort of deafened inner ear,
A dumb man telling us to go
Or asking, worse, *why are you here?*
In syllables of sudden fear –
The sort of thing that scares a crow.

A conversation burning low,
A smoking wick, a sooty smear,
Dark corners out of which might peer
A truth that we shall never know.
There used to be a chandelier
And hanging from it with a sneer
A dumb man telling us to go.

A silence full of fallen snow,
An emptiness from far to near,
Then something poking like a spear,
The sort of thing that scares a crow;
A black box with a built-in veer,
A caw not sounding quite sincere,
A truth that we shall never know.

Guides and good shepherds here below
– but now the rhyme begins to blur –
A soulless psycho-engineer,
A dumb man telling us to go,
A blind man teaching us to steer,
And then that crippled mountaineer,
The sort of thing that scares a crow.

A great negation drowns our 'No'.
This ocean where we reach no shore
Was charted by a gondolier.
A truth that we shall never know
Is washed away as mermaids cheer
At wrecks and rocks and disappear.
A dumb man telling us to go

Does it with gestures showing how
To make a bonfire of the year
And pile up in a triple tier
The sort of thing that scares a crow,
A truth that we shall never know,
A dumb man telling us to go.

Eleven Little Poems

big muse
big time
little muse
all the time

I   *Walking Out of the World*

Like the long hill
And at the top
I stand quite still

II   *In the Mouth*

Teeth to which other teeth were fixed
Teeth on which other teeth were hung
Are drawn and gone and leave unmixed
A total triumph to the tongue.

III   *As Per Contract*

East wind and icy moon and still you smile.
Poems silenced, worlds destroyed; I know my place
In the void, my way in the dark. And still I see your face
Smiling as you smiled; not gentle in dismissal.

IV   *Grown-ups*

We know now how they watched
From a seat in the evening shade
As we raced untiring into the
                       last of day;
How they saw us run free, for ever,
Playing beyond that mortal shade
In which they sat, arms strong,
                       hands adroit.

V   *I.M. Francis Albert*

All the love songs.

You are dead. Frank.

Someone must
go on singing.

This chap sounds
as if his voice was
broken at birth.

VI   *The Reign*

How will she rule?

With wit and beauty.

And when the crowsfeet
Tread her eyes, and when
Her shafts are only cruel?

She rules. The air is bright about her.

VII   *From the German*

A spectre is haunting Germany –
The spectre of Germany.

VIII   *Triolet with Knockout Back-Axle*

Wasn't the route to take
Indivisible load
A humpty we didn't make
Wasn't the route to take
A silly sodding mistake
Jammed tight across the road
Wasn't the route to take
Indivisible load.

ix   A Note for the Next Stranger

She did not know me.

Wordless in
nameless nowhere
I claim non-recognition
as my own.

I go to that dark
from this dark

where she will not know you.

x   Report

There is no mystery in man
than no confession left unsaid
than veils of terror torn apart.

The best plan is to have no plan –
all the bright horrors of the head
light the dark secrets of the heart.

XI *Than to Arrive*

Lamed by a long hard march I hobble in,
Reporting my arrival with a salami-breath –
The unexpired portion of the day's ration
    eaten and forgotten
Except for the belch which might teach dead Hungarians
    a little more about death.

The First Cold Mornings

A biting wind snaps up the street
And autumn lies around in shreds,
Farmers are sowing winter wheat
But almost naked from their beds

Girls dawdle like a summer dream
To parky corners for a bus
Or open-coated sway and stream
(snug in their subcutaneous)

Down cold-iron platforms. You and I
Shiver to see them – tights and blouse,
Bra, skirt, what else? A bluish thigh
And we kit up for Arctic days:

Wool underpants, wool topcoat, wool
Layer on layer round the chest;
A kind of displaced Russian swaddle.
They felt us freezing as they dressed –

Who in their man-made fibres dare
This eastern wind, this northern light,
Still wrapt in that still tropic air
Which warmed the chilly sheets last night.

With a Styptic Pencil

Once again God's day is dawning.
We are tired but we shall rise,
White and spiteful, hairy, yawning,
Night and nothing in our eyes,

Men like beasts but born of woman,
False to all but flesh and blood,
We shall face the day with doom on –
Beast like man like manlike god:

Stubble, blood and sticking plaster,
Shaky hand and sacred task,
Men as empty as disaster
Glare from mirrors like a mask;

Men as cold as all creation,
Men conceived by no mistake,
Stare in after-shaved elation
Proud to find the form they take.

We shall live our lives in terror,
Unoriginals of sin.
God, like nothing in a mirror,
Feels a day of ours begin.

Bearings

It takes a blonde to break your heart.
A lean brunette will get you down.
A redhead turn and hate the sight
Of something she could tear apart.
The other girls will only bite.
A lean brunette will get you down.
It takes a blonde to break your heart.

Triolet

Young girls explode with things to say.
An older woman means the most.
Her calm assurance points the way
(Young girls explode with things to say)
To light the fuse to stir the clay –
A depth-charge like the Holy Ghost.
[(Young girls explode with things to say)]
An older woman means the most.

In That Wild Bed

She conceives more than the child.

Time and death safe in the womb
She measures meaning like an untold tale.
The dream of man men do not dream
Beguiles her afternoons, sunlight
Reveals a purpose that men do not dare.

She is to sit at the centre of the hearth
Making new only what is to be told again
To children round the bright fire, honour-bright.

Till the Sands of the Desert

Small-fingered, famine-pale,
Clasped in a smudge of dusk,
She stilled a hunger for eternity
No dawn renews though dawns enough have dawned
And in the twinkling of no time at all
Approximations-to-the-goddess-once
Stare up at towering sons;
Full days, adulteries, the fatter years.

Yet what once so undid him,
Cool-fingered, harem-eyed,
Persists in mercy. Smiling through the shade
She pledges still to be all that redeems him now –
Stripping him down to what he is:
One wife's plump passion.

Too Late for the Centenary

e e cummings: 94 to 94

missed it
the day –
14 october –
missed it
the year

the blind
lead the
blind now

you are
herstory now

(and again)

you are

the hot tip
of
immortality

looking up
from the lap
of dark down

at your name
in lights on
the nipple

this is for ever

suck it and see.

15 October 95

Mermaids: One

The wave's caress,
the long haul of lithe water,
breasts breasting the foam.

Slight, salty kisses;
flash of limbless
limbs from the depth;
the shore drenched
with a breathless gasp;
dark, depthless eyes.

It is splash and sun
in the shallows;
they will not drown you now.

Mermaids: Two

The arms of winding water
twist and embrace in cold blood,
thighless thighs bump in their element.

The sky is open
and the sea is deep;
a last look, a last breath,
down we go,
bruise and ooze,
tasting them forever.

Their dark eyes open,
they themselves
dive not to drown.

In the Bleachery

I

a yellow of yellow grins,
lips twisting to frame
the denture;

a red
of sunset
after sunset;

blue,
black
with thunder –

primary colours
lived in the drench
of light, died
with the light.

II

a yellow
of toothless
grins;

red of a sun
unrisen;

blue of the
blind eye –

now come the counter-colours,
into breath-thin air,
darkening the darkness.

Low Blood Pressure

If death were life I could not die.
If life were death I need not live;
Unburied by necessity
Beneath a bony negative

Death would be death and I as dead
As now I live my life alive –
Mortal with nothing left to dread,
Undying only to survive.

Her quick lungs gulp the empty air,
Her bright eyes scan the barren land.
Night was a lover never there,
Day is a cold and empty hand.

One day within a living breath
The dead will never lie alone,
One day deep down in life and death,
One day when life and death are one.

Kenneth Cain

'... the squads will be armed
with airguns and bows
and arrows ...'
Kenneth Cain
at ten
telling me
at ten
Kenneth Cain
hair no fairer
than mine
but with a curl
Kenneth Cain
expounder of straightforward
fantasy

Kenneth Cain
armed as a pilot
Fleet Air Arm
killed as a pilot
Kenneth Cain

After the Break

The time left hers
and all again in order;
we wait as we must wait –
the unborn
to be born,
the undead
still to die.

Hers hour by hour
and dark by dark
the fearless metaphor:
eternity black as night

where guided we shall go
the unborn
to their birth
the undead
to their dying.

There being no brighter eyes.

The Drill

I smelt this silence
in the salt dark
before dawn,
tasted it in the small-talk
of parting – touch and tremble:
earth heart bough
shake ache break.

So that as I go,
ceasing to be,
a silent world
untouched, untasted,
will be not what I relinquish
but what I move to meet.

It is like this.
Senseless.
You are not there.
My hands hold nothing.

open the book close the book

Help the Aged

She is what she was, she returns,
wholly possessing repletion,
emptying afternoon
of sunlight and pale clutter;
sated visions move with her –
that was the day then, this is the dusk;
soon she will walk in darkness.

II

I am the little old chap
with white hair and palms like parchment
at the end of the back row
of the twentieth century
staring into the dark

III

A girl, a moth, a dying flame.
A man who does not know his name.

His puzzled stare, his fondled fear,
His sense of nothing coming near.

Her heart is dark, her realm is night.
She comes again to light the light.

You in Your Small Corner

empty heart and empty head
empty eyes that look away
unturned pages left unread
nothing more or less to say

wall to left and wall to right
chair behind a table-top
eyes that watch the day for night
hours that wait for time to stop

noise and news from far and now
sounds unheard and sounds uncanned
breast-beat like a broken vow
base-note like a lost command

deafen but do not define
what an empty heart is for
nor an empty head like mine

sit alone and say no more.

At the Turn

A century of disaster; ours –
I face the future like a slave
Denied a master's easy terrors.
An era like a common grave

For men with early deaths to die
Crossing four hundred yards of mud.
Exploding on a tracered sky
A lot of God went west for good.

A clammy, corpse-like kind of past,
A present sense of days long-doomed
To leave a man alone at last
Feeling like something just exhumed.

A life got up, a zombie fake.
A universe of scattered ash.
Ache scar weal whip/whip weal scar ache.
I go on when I feel the lash.

Losses 2002

'... you three boys ...'

Norman
(youngest)
10 January
Hamilton
New Zealand

Dennis
(midmost)
2 March
Croxley Green
England

leaving me
(eldest)
dateless
nowhere

Karfreitag

The Hag

She came out of an alley
into a busy street and her eyes,
plucking my face from the many
passing faces, measured me with a look
– and the cackle of her derision
  drowned in a grate of gears.

I heard her laughter.
I have not turned back.
I should not refuse oblivion.

The Space Where I Stood

Look and you will not see me,
I could not remain where I was,
I left my place in time

wishing neither to go nor to stay
nor to be somewhere else –
there are journeys beyond desire.

No other place, no other time;
the dull mirror is blank –
look, you will not see me.

Absence, presence – I was a little man
on his way to nowhere. She dances
the pattern of being

in the shape of dusk; I watched
my part in that pattern, I could not
remain where I was. Look there at a time and place

where I no longer watch; infinite space
fills the clearing
of that lost inch and hour.

I am measured by that measure.

The Sentences of Death

NINE ASPECTS
OF A SYNDROME

'To be taken to the place from which you came ...'

One: *Set Up*

The night is lit
as eternity
will be lit

Muse
silver shadow
Moon
silver substance

Now death is dumb

No dark sayings
dreary
the night
with dreams
of dawn
No sweaty echoes
of a broken vow
shake down
the stars

The night is lit
once and for all:
dead or alive
the night is no man's now

Moon
your leafless
windless silver

Muse
the silver
of your silence

The night is lit
for eternity
Shadow and substance
share the silver bed:
this is as good as death

There is no rhyme
for silver.

Two: *Death as a Foreign Language, Lesson One*

You will die
He will die
She will die
They will die

You are dying
He is dying
She is dying
They are dying

You shall die
He shall die
bunion
onion
She shall die
They shall die

You are dead
Twentyfour
Sixtyfour
He she they
are dead

They are the dead

In a short time
the pupil will be saying:

'a dead man
and a moonless sky'
or be pronouncing:
'the faint stale glitter ...'

An easy language to learn.
Simple to translate.

Three: *Cowardice in Face of the Blank Page*

Words fall from lipless lips, leaves fall from leafless trees;
a bare branch, a gallows, sky a hollow socket
unstaring from a skull; echoes of guilty pleas,
claims to the right to die, fill corridor and court.

To become no one again and nothing again,
to revert to the inert start, to the cold lump
of clay crumbling to dust out on the great plain
beyond knowing, past caring, before the high jump

of forever grounded forever and no day;
no word audible, unsaid, lipless lips, unheard,
these are the leafless leaves falling, this is the way
silence begins and ends, pitiless and absurd.

You will not hear though you think you hear or could hear
if you were near enough to hear – calls of farewell
torn to whispers by a wind; high-pitched cries of fear
stifled, cushioned; interminable tales still to tell

but not to be told. You did not miss what was said
for nothing was said. You need not misunderstand
Death saying nothing (except perhaps to the dead).

There is no distant drum, no anthem, no lost land.
You will hear nothing. Do not listen until you must.
Black-capped Death believes all sentences are just.

Four: *Local Colour Seen as Camouflage*

Walking about Bad Godesberg
Waiting to die: up the hill
To the woods, through the woods,
Down the hill past the empty shops,
Past the empty department store
– when the government goes
this will be a ghost town
and I shall be a ghost.

Walking through Bad Godesberg
Waiting for death
– 'of which we know nothing' –
Strolling through town
Down the avenue to the river.

If the Rhine were the Styx
I could take the Dollendorfer ferry
– a cheerful Charon here –
To the Deadland of Niederdollendorf
And walk south through the Hades
Of Königswinter and return
on the slow Königswinterer ferry
– a sullen crew there –
To this Left Bank and Mehlem

And all would be known
– '. . . bloke back from the dead' –

The Hotel Dreesen looks up.
The Hotel Petersberg looks down.

Five: *And Daylight Hours Tomorrow*

Suicide weather
slack and dull
wrapped like a sack
around the skull
Melancholia
gnaws the bone
dine together
die alone

Just the weather
for suicide
blind and blank
like a self denied
Day was a wank
and night a nigger
a rotting rope
and a rusty trigger

Suicide weather
cold and cruel
end of a tether
end of it all
Bloody final
a soul uptight
phantomising
the real dark night.

Slack and dull
blind and blank
cold and cruel.

Six: *In the Epitaph Section*

Skull-sleep:
All that is left
Is more than we thought.

Skeleton-stretch:
Words on a page
In a closed book,
Words on a stone
In nowhere.

Bone fingers fumble
For the place,
Finding the words.

Read them as the dead read;
Let the sockets see.

Seven: *Drill for a Deathbed*

Face death
Turn to the wall
Death has no face
no fingers to touch
no hand to take
no eyes to meet
Turn to the wall

Dead or alive
as real or unreal
as you ever were
Turn to the wall
Face death
Now the man who was
not killed then
dies now

Death does not want
to be faced
nor to be understood
Turn to the wall
Death has learned no language

Look away
Face the wall
Do not wait for words.

Eight: *Sitrep*

The dead are safely dead.
We still have risks to take.
A hazard for each head.
The dead are safely dead.
Blockhead and loggerhead
Our hearts will ache and break.
The dead are safely dead.
We still have risks to take

And promises to break.
The dead are true to death,
We still have time to fake
And promises to break
And so for no one's sake
We draw another breath.
Unsworn to ache and break
The dead are true to death.

We shall lie safe and true
In undawns yet to break
No dying left to do
We shall lie safe and true
As doubly dead and two
With nothing to forsake
We shall lie safe and true
In undawns yet to break.

The dead are safe and sure.
We flinch and fear the dark
And names that mean no more.
The dead are safe and sure.
Water from shore to shore
And nowhere to embark.
The dead are safe and sure.
We flinch and fear the dark.

The dead are safely dead.
The dead are true to death.
The dead are safe and sure.

Nine: *Fade Out*

The night is lit
cunningly

Her eyes meet his
his arms hold her

Shadows,
they kiss in the shadow

They are lit
for the final scene
and eternity
(silver and silver)
This is their moment
monumental
they clutch forever

There will be nothing
after this
No proof that
you were her
or I was he
No rhyme for silver

A small night music
ends. Death follows
dark and dumb.
Like a man in love.

This is no place for us.